My Life As A Cigarette Lighter

By

Cath Cunningham

My Life As A Cigarette Lighter

Published in Australia by: FirstPage Press

Cover design by FirstPage Press

Edited by FirstPage Press

Printed in Australia

Paper Back.

E-Book.

Hard Back.

Table of Contents

Chapter 1:
Conception

I thought the earth had fallen apart. Certainly, I just about did! An eardrum-shattering BANG, a retina-searing flash of light, a slightly toxic odour and taste, all accompanied by a bolt of fear that coursed through every part of my being, leaving me trembling and shaking. Confused and dazed, I became aware of a warm, glowing flame emanating from my head. As the light I was creating from within shone brightly above, I was filled with immense knowledge and understanding. I knew what I was! I knew I had just come to life! I knew I had a purpose and was useful! I was a very proud blue Bic cigarette lighter, and it was my job to light as many cigarettes as I could. I would take on this responsibility with great commitment and dedication. Ready to fire up at a moment's notice, I would fulfil my mission well throughout my life, reliable and steadfast. Like all Bic lighters, I would live up to the reputation of 'just one flick with a Bic'! I would…

"Yep, these ones are good to go!" shouted the man who had facilitated my awakening, simultaneously and unceremoniously throwing me into a box of other newborn cigarette lighters.

"Have you checked them all?" boomed some other voice.

"Yeah, I already told you, they're right to go! How many times do I have to say it?"

As the two voices argued back and forth, I settled into my new environment. To the left, right, and below me was a sea of colours, a cacophony of noise, and a great deal of movement as all the baby cigarette lighters chatted excitedly about the futures they envisaged for themselves. Blackness suddenly enveloped us as the lid was closed and taped shut. We were all jammed in together. We were heading for the next chapter in our lives: Distribution! And were we excited!!!

Chapter 2:
Distribution

For the next few weeks, not much happened for us fledgling cigarette lighters, filled with our own self-importance. Jammed inside our box, we had little to occupy us, save contemplating our futures. Sometimes our temporary home was still for lengthy periods. Sometimes we were on the move. To where, we could only wonder.

At one point, we had been stationary for a while when the completely unexpected happened. Our lovely, cosy, safe box that had protected us in our travels to date was picked up, dropped onto a counter (we all got headaches), and brutally opened with a knife!

That's right! We all got such a fright, bedazzled by the light as we were, and proceeded to fall out of the split in the side of the box (caused by the knife being poorly operated) and spill out onto the counter and even onto the floor. The knife-wielding maniac used language fit for a sailor when he saw us scattered everywhere. Complaining loudly, he proceeded to pick us all up and place us upright on a shelf in what could loosely be described as a shop. Exactly what type of shop, I never did determine.

I was one of the unfortunates who landed on the floor, meaning I now had twice the headache I had received from the counter collision! The upside, though, was that I was one of the last to be picked up and therefore positioned in the front row of all the lighters, with a clear view of the establishment and an excellent chance of being quickly selected for adoption! Soon I would be lighting cigarettes one after the other! I couldn't wait!

I was quite curious about the nature of this business. The shop (if it warranted the name) seemed severely understocked. Bare shelves were the norm, with a smattering of cheap, tacky trinkets occasionally on display throughout. There were garish, lighted signs reading 'welcome' or 'open', flickering on and off to the right. The light from these gave the appearance of a mini disco happening in one corner.

Meanwhile, years of accumulated dust and grime had settled on everything, except us recent arrivals. I could see that if I wasn't sold soon, I'd start to take on the same dull appearance as the stock I saw before my eyes.

We were all worried about this possibility, worried that our shiny newness would quickly fade in this lifeless premises. We were also worried that we may not be bought and would live out our days perched atop the shelf, and we worried because when a customer did come in, he or she was never interested in anything in the shop. The routine was: a customer would enter the shop and go straight to the counter. No browsing, no even glancing at the stock. The customer would then mutter something to the owner, who would disappear into the back room. The owner would return with a bag, take money from the customer, and the transaction would be complete. The customer would leave without so much as a glance in our direction, and our collective disappointment was palpable.

Then, one day, the unexpected happened.

A young man, donning the ever-popular jeans and hoodie, entered the shop, approached the counter, spoke to the man, and waited patiently while the owner went out the back. The owner returned with the bag, money changed hands, and the youth went to leave, when he stopped.

"Hey, you wouldn't have any cigarette lighters, would you?" the youth asked.

"Sure! What colour?" came the reply.

"Blue!" I couldn't believe my luck! Not only was I blue, I was also the ONLY blue cigarette lighter in the front row!

The owner reached up. I felt his warm hand wrap around me. Next thing, I was briefly in another hand and then in the bag the young man had bought.

I could hear my friends wishing me well (some a little enviously) as I bounced in the bag, out of the shop and into my new life. Soon, so soon, I would be living in all my glory…

Chapter 3:
A Place to Call Home

It felt like we'd been walking forever, my new, youthful friend and I bouncing our way along our route towards the great unknown. My friend's gait was somewhat erratic and unsteady, and he seemed to be in quite a hurry. I didn't mind being transported like this, as I had a soft bed of slightly damp, green stuff to land on. It was very comfy, but it stank to high heaven. I had a fair idea the stuff was for smoking, and I became very excited at the thought of lighting my friend's cigarettes.

After what seemed like an eternity, we stopped, and I heard a key being slid into a lock and a door opened. We walked inside to the accompanying sounds of voices calling out,

"Did you get it?"

"About time! Where have you been?"

"Yeah, I got it," my friend retorted. "Calm down! I remembered the lighter too!" He opened the bag, extracted me from my bed, and waved me in the air as evidence. I just had time for a quick glance around the room before being placed on a table littered with objects.

Along one wall was a couch. This had clearly seen better days. A relic from the 70s, the original bright orange had long faded to a dull tan, spotted with stains from innumerable sources. The vinyl had ripped in places, and it was apparent that many lit cigarette butts had, over the years, been dropped on that couch. I knew I'd come home!

Three more young male specimens adorned the couch, all attired similarly, and all much more interested in the contents of the bag than in me. The remainder of the room housed a milk crate (doubling as a seat), an electric bar heater with exposed wires that probably shouldn't have been in use, a broken vacuum cleaner abandoned by its previous owner, and the coffee table on which I now found myself. Technically, I suppose this piece of furniture could not really be called a coffee table, although it served the same function. It was actually an old door, balancing on bricks, somewhat precariously.

Scattered across the 'table' was an assortment of empty chip packets, soft drink cans, lollie wrappers, and other food packaging, the contents eaten. There were sticky patches where drinks had been spilt, left to evaporate and gather enough dust that the stickiness was minimised. At least, that was both the plan and the practice. The overflow from the 'table' was on the floor: empty pizza cartons, Macca's and Hungry Jack's logos aplenty, gracing the antiquated, threadbare carpet and making movement around the room problematic. I found it all a bit depressing, but I was optimistic about my future and didn't let it get to me.

In a surprisingly rubbish-free space, I had been placed next to some objects, which I then directed my attention to: a dirty bowl housing the dregs of a tobacco pouch, some equally dirty scissors, a stained and filthy homemade bong constructed from a discarded plastic Coke bottle and the obligatory garden hose, and a dying black cigarette lighter.

The latter, struggling with dangerously low energy, had ceased to be of use to our human companions and was probably destined for the floor. He had been hanging on as long as possible until his replacement arrived. Now I was here, he could quietly slip away. His work was done. He told me that his only regret was that he hadn't lit many cigarettes of late. Three months ago it was all he did, but in recent times all he'd done was fire up the bong. The boys now preferred spending their money on marijuana rather than tobacco. "Sure," he reminisced, "one of them will occasionally smoke a cigarette, but it's rare. It's usually just bong after bong after bong, and it's not what I was created for!"

I really felt his pain and could empathise with his suffering. But his words worried me… what if I was destined to spend my life in this squalor, only ever lighting bongs? This was not part of my plan. I wanted to travel and, as a cigarette lighter, this was a possibility. Friday night drinks at the pub, guess who'd be invited along? Morning smoko at work, I'd definitely be needed then. Who knows? I might even be taken on a holiday, the possibilities were endless.

Instead, it looked like I'd be cooped up on the coffee table next to the bong, bowl and scissors until either I died or there was a police raid. I was doomed…

I turned to offer the words I thought a dying cigarette lighter would want to hear, but realised he'd gone. His energy had died. His gas had run out. In some ways, cigarette lighters are like humans: filled to the brim with energy and vitality when they're young, still quite active in middle age, with a gradual slowing down towards the end of life. Like humans, we become less reliable as our body parts age and our internal life force diminishes. When we're young, one flick and we're lit, us Bics! As our gas store ebbs away, it can become harder and harder to light first time, sometimes requiring half a dozen clicks to get a flame. That's when you know your days are numbered.

Me though, I was at the start of my life, only ignited once, and ready to dazzle the boys with my brilliance! Even if it was only with a bong.

While I had been perusing my new surrounds and their various occupants, the young men had started preparing the mixing bowl, blending the slightly damp marijuana with the bone-dry tobacco shards. There wasn't much tobacco, which had me concerned. See, unlike a cigarette, which on a wind-free day could confidently be lit in under two seconds, keeping damp marijuana smouldering was going to use a lot of my energy. Especially when there were four of them, all taking turns! I'd planned a long and celebrated life, lighting cigarettes and travelling around, and things were clearly not going to plan! Still, I reasoned with myself, things could be worse: I could be at the back of the shelf, stuck in the shop. I decided to put my best foot forward.

Having packed the bong, the first of the three on the couch picked me up, leaned forward over the mouthpiece, hair draping gracefully, forming a tent over me and the apparatus, and proceeded to flick the Bic. Me, confident in my ability to ignite the cherry, burst forth in a rush of youthful exuberance, withholding nothing.

The top of my flame took out all of his right eyelashes and most of that eyebrow. The tent largely disintegrated around me instantly, leaving a smouldering stubble for a fringe and a disgusting smell in the air. The accompanying expletives were very colourful.

Things settled down and he tried again, this time with greater success, no doubt in part because my earlier enthusiasm had waned and, besides, he had no more front hair left. I felt deep shame. The very first thing I had lit in my life had not been a cigarette. It had not even been a bong. It had been a human's hair! I was mortified. I was also deeply grateful that no other cigarette lighter had witnessed my failure. The babies were still in the shop and the old lighter was dead.

Round and round the bong and I were passed, and I was just starting to get the hang of it when my original friend said he had to deliver some of the product to his cousin, who lived several suburbs away. The others showed little interest in his movements until he mentioned he would be taking me with him so the others couldn't smoke any more in his absence. A brief argument ensued, but my friend got his way, pocketing both me and a quantity of marijuana. I was overjoyed as we headed for the train station.

On board, we settled into a seat on a fairly overcrowded train. Sitting next to us was a woman nursing a very active toddler. The kid was sitting on the woman's lap, facing her. He squirmed frequently and his foot kept kicking my friend in the upper thigh, right near the pocket I was in. I think my friend was about to say something when the carriage door opened to reveal two ticket inspectors entering the area, flashing badges and demanding to see tickets. Two things happened: one, my friend tensed his body (he didn't have a ticket), causing me to push up towards the opening of his pocket, and two, the kid kicked at just the right moment and with just the right force to send me hurtling out of the pocket, down the side of the thigh and ending up wedged between my friend's seat and the woman's seat.

I was stuck! I watched with dismay and a sense of powerlessness as the ticket inspectors escorted my friend from the train, leaving me alone and more than a little bit afraid…

Chapter 4:
Travelling Through Life

I was jammed! Wedged tight between two seats that, over the course of the day, had witnessed numerous backsides making contact. Any time someone took their seat, I was pushed further and further down the gap between the seats until I was nearly at floor level. My future looked grim. However, throughout the day, I was actually travelling. I was going all across this vast city's train network, hearing the names of suburbs as the recorded message announced the stations and feeling movement as passengers were variously disgorged from the train or swallowed into its cavernous interior at each stop. I liked the swaying movement of the train and the representatives of humanity gathered within. However, the view was terrible! Whoever designed the fabric covering the seats was clearly working to a budget. Drab, unexciting colours formed the basis for a repetitive pattern of geometric shapes. Anything more than a glance promised excruciating boredom… and I was stuck, glued in position, staring at the most mundane image in recorded history. And so the hours passed…

Eventually the train spat out the last of its passengers and the empty carriages were parked in a siding. There we remained for another two days.

My earlier optimism was rapidly disappearing, as something akin to despair began to settle in. This was probably worse than being at the back of the shelf in the shop. At least there were some limited forms of life in that environment. Here, in the train, there was no life. It felt like all the oxygen had been suctioned out of the space when the lights were extinguished and, from my vantage point, there was nothing but blackness and silence. It was hell! And my mind played havoc with me, imagining scenes of being rescued, only to have my hopes shattered when the reality of my situation came crashing in. I was sinking fast.

At one point I heard the sound of doors opening, but figured it was just a new hallucination and ignored it. More sounds joined the doors, footsteps, the rustle of clothing as someone moved about, and finally some kind of machinery, presumably used for cleaning. I ignored them all, confident that I was getting a grip on the delusions and successfully managing them. That was until the employee ID plastic card bashed me on the head, having fallen through the gap between the seats and now cosily jammed between me and one of the seats.

"Ow!" I said crossly, quickly followed by the strange question, "Are you real?"

"Of course I'm real," replied the ID card. "And so is she."

"Who's she?" I asked, feeling stupid.

"My human, of course! She's dropped me again and now I'm lost. She needs to fix the clip on her lanyard, but she keeps forgetting to. I've been lost heaps of times, but she always finds me. She's OK. A hard worker and a single mother of five. She cleans the trains to give her kids a decent life. She's always tired and stressed, so I forgive her when she loses me."

"Do you think she'll find you this time? Do you think she might find me too?" I asked wistfully, as a spark of hope was ignited.

Just then the tips of fingers appeared above us, gingerly feeling their way down to our resting place. The fingers touched the card, inadvertently pushing it further towards the ground. This action, however, resulted in me being positioned *above* the card, almost ensuring my escape! The fingertips touched my surface and, a short while later, both the card and I were in our rescuer's hand and, while the card and lanyard were reunited, I was first tested to check I worked, and then slid into a pocket.

My travelling had recommenced…

Chapter 5:
Home, sweet home

Nestled securely in the woman's pocket, I chatted with the ID card as the woman drove home. The woman had five children, aged between 15 and 3. She had been raising them alone ever since the card had known her, some 18 months. She was a hard worker, a bit of a perfectionist, and highly valued by her employer for her thoroughness and attention to detail. Similarly, her home environment was kept to a high standard, given her numerous offspring. The children were, by and large, well behaved. Her middle child, Tommy, 12 years old, gave her the greatest grief. He hated school, was disinterested in sports and had no hobbies to speak of. Tommy took the absence of his father the hardest of all the children and his behaviour often reflected his confused and turbulent emotional state. Tommy believed himself responsible for his parents' separation and, filled with self-contempt, had recently joined a small gang of kids who escaped life's tedium by getting up to mischief. Some of the gang's activities had drawn the attention of the local constabulary, which had the woman worried. Tommy was a good kid at heart, but was going astray under the influence of the gang's leaders.

"Yep, Tommy's the one you're going to have to watch. Who knows what he might get up to with you?" cautioned the ID card. I didn't really care much about the children, including Tommy. I was more interested in the woman and whether she smoked or not. Eventually, the card paused long enough in the recitation for me to ask my pressing question, to which I got the reply, "No, she doesn't smoke." I was immensely disappointed with the news and the card, trying to cheer me up, said, "She doesn't smoke, but I reckon Tommy does. He's your best bet!" I determined to pay Tommy as much attention as I could.

The following few weeks passed uneventfully. The woman had placed me on the top shelf of the pantry and, when the door was open, I could see the kitchen, dining area and a bit of the lounge. Even when the door was closed, I could still hear what was going on. The home was warm, cosy, generally tidy, yet very much lived in. I was happy here, with lots of entertainment, but something was missing. I had no job, no role, no purpose. My hopes of being an exemplary cigarette lighter were fading fast.

Christmas was rapidly approaching and as the house was being rearranged and decorated to accommodate the festive season, plans were underway for the big day. A traditional Christmas lunch was on the menu and the guest list included extended family. The woman's parents, her brother and his family would all be in attendance. Being a sole parent with limited income, her parents had offered to purchase the meat for the meal, her brother and his wife were bringing all the vegetables and trimmings, while she provided the venue and the all-important plum pudding. The house was abuzz with excitement!

Christmas morning was a noisy affair, as the grandparents arrived early to take photos of the children opening their presents. "Not too early to put the meat on?" queried the woman's father once the last present had been opened.

"Well, the Weber is going to have to heat up before we can start roasting any of the meat, so it might as well be gotten underway. Heat beads and firelighters are in the laundry cupboard."

"Righto!" came the reply as the father ambled off to undertake the task.

"You got anything to light it with?" said the returning father, querying his daughter. "Sure Dad! I picked up an old cigarette lighter at work recently. Lucky! Don't know if I've got any matches and the shops are all closed!"

This statement was met with a mixed response from Yours Truly. Firstly, I was quite indignant at being called 'old'. I was actually very young still! Secondly, and this overrode my indignation, I was going to be useful and be put to work. Lighting cigarettes didn't look promising, but at least I'd be doing something!

The woman collected me from my vantage point, handing me to her father. Outside at the BBQ, the heat beads had been neatly arranged, dotted with cubes of firelighters. It was a bit overkill actually, but I performed my role magnificently and soon a hearty fire was underway. Fire lit, the father absent-mindedly left me on a small side table, home to various cooking implements. I had a good view of the backyard and was quite content, lying in the morning sun, just watching the world go by.

Out of the corner of my eye, I could see Tommy. I wondered why he was hiding behind the lemon tree. He seemed to be looking at the house, then the BBQ, then back to the house. Suddenly, and quite purposefully, he strode across the backyard to the table, hesitated, took one final glance at the house and I was in his pocket. I was overjoyed. All my Christmases had come at once. Finally, I was going to get to light a cigarette!

Chapter 6:
Trouble

Christmas lunch passed uneventfully. Much food, drink and laughter traversed the lips of the assembled family members. By 3 pm, the dishes were done, the brother and his family had departed to celebrate Christmas dinner elsewhere, and the remaining three adults were relaxing, semi-comatose, in the lounge with the air conditioner on. The children were alternating between playing with their toys and taking turns on the Slip n Slide, a gift from their grandparents. Tommy, in whose pocket I had spent the past few hours, was talking to a friend on the phone. They were planning a meet-up for the gang at the basketball courts in the school grounds.

"Now is a good time," advised the young voice over the phone's speaker. "All the adults are too busy getting drunk and fighting with each other to notice what we're doing. See you in 10 minutes. I'll let the others know. Don't forget to bring the lighter."

"It's in my pocket," Tommy informed the voice.

"Mum, can I go for a ride to the shops?" Tommy asked, breezing into the lounge with its dozing occupants.

"The shops are shut, Tommy, and besides, it's too hot!"

"I'll be right, Mum. The wind will keep me cool, I want to try out my new helmet and I'll take a water bottle with me. Please?"

"Oh alright, but ride along George Street and through the park, where there's plenty of shade."

"OK, Mum!" And just like that, we were on our way.

We sailed along, and as predicted, the wind provided some relief from the heat, but we were minus the water bottle. We were also in the blazing sun and I could feel dampness enveloping me as Tommy's pores broke out in an increasingly heavy sweat.

Meanwhile, I could barely contain my excitement. My imagination led me to wild places, of 20 children all needing to light their cigarettes. I would be in huge demand. Everyone would be wanting my assistance. I would be so popular. This was exactly what I had been created for. At long last!

We arrived at the basketball courts to the warm greetings of a couple of kids on bikes. "The others are already at the storage shed, hiding out the back. They've got everything else, have you got the lighter?"

"Sure have!" answered Tommy. "I stole it from my Mum."

"Good one! Let's go."

During the ride to the storage shed, I worried that I was stolen property and thus party to a crime. But my delight at being a proper cigarette lighter overshadowed my concerns. Arriving at the back of the shed, I was both surprised and disappointed that there were only two additional members of the gang present. Where were all the others?

And where, more importantly, were the cigarettes? I had a quick look around, but the area seemed to be void of tobacco products.

I noticed the shed, wooden, with peeling paint. I noticed the way the wind had blown leaf and tree litter up against the back wall of the shed. I noticed one of the assembled picking up a can and pouring liquid on the leaves. I smelt the petrol!

"Oh, no, no, no, no, no!" I thought.

"You have to light it, Tommy! It's your lighter and besides, if you do this, you will become an official 'Carnage' member."

"Can't someone else do it? I might not do it right..."

"You'll be fine, Tommy. Just do it!"

Tommy's tentative steps took him to the edge of the accumulated tree debris. He slowly bent down, extended his arm and ignited me.

One second I was doing my job, burning a nice little flame, the next I was flying through the air, separated from Tommy, over a fence, and landing on a neighbouring property, which backed onto the school grounds. I lay there stunned, hearing Tommy's cries of pain, caused both by burns he had sustained and by the injuries he was receiving as his friends dragged him across fairly rough terrain and away from the blaze. Clouds and clouds of thick, black smoke filled the air as the flames quickly devoured the building and all its contents. As the sound of the boys trailed away, a siren could be heard approaching. A couple of fire trucks valiantly battled the flames, but it was a lost cause. The old building didn't have a hope, especially on such a windy, hot day. The fire personnel ignored the building, turning their attention to the nearby trees and fences. If this took off, an adjacent nature reserve could be next, and then houses and lost lives could follow.

It would be a terrible Christmas Day.

A couple of police cars had arrived, mainly for crowd control at that stage, although they would later attempt to locate any witnesses to the events.

While all the action was taking place, the owner of the property where I had recently taken up residence arrived, garden hose in hand. He proceeded to hose his wooden fence, managing to save it from more than a scorching. At one point, he stepped on me. Lifting the offensive foot, he spotted me on the grass. He bent down and, careful to handle only my ends, slid me into a pocket of his shorts. Eventually, he handed me to the boss cop, who carted me off as evidence. Great! Now I was under arrest.

Chapter 7:
Behind bars

His badge told me he was Senior Sergeant Robert McKenzie. His badge, which talked a lot, also told me Senior Sergeant Robert McKenzie was renowned for his short temper and overall nasty demeanour. His badge also reported that Senior Sergeant Robert McKenzie was in an extremely foul mood currently. This last piece of information was not exactly news to me. Aggression and possible violence lurked in the man's eyes. His stare made me question his sanity.

Driving back to the station, he almost hit an elderly couple out on the street, watching the commotion, so hell-bent was he on seeing justice done to whoever had ruined his Christmas. He had a fair idea who was responsible. What had started as childish pranks conducted by this gang had today escalated to arson. He had been trying for almost a year to get sufficient evidence against these children to have them sent away. He didn't care where, just as long as they were out of his jurisdiction. One in particular was definitely heading for gaol, with a couple of older siblings already doing time.

As far as Senior Sergeant Robert McKenzie was concerned, the judicial system had gone to the dogs. Soft magistrates with bleeding hearts repeatedly showed leniency to young hoodlums, with little repercussion for crimes committed.

But this time, he was backing a winner, he was sure. Human life had been potentially endangered and if he could just lift some prints off the lighter, he might at least be able to nail this incident on one of them, who would hopefully dob the rest in. But he needed those prints urgently.

Senior Sergeant Robert McKenzie had such a vendetta against the children that he had decided to personally oversee their demise. Thus, any activity suspected of being the work of 'his' gang was automatically referred to him. Despite not being rostered on for

Christmas Day, his staff had no hesitation calling him when the fire was first reported. Indeed, he would have been furious had they not. He was angry, not at his staff, but at the little bastards who had to pick Christmas Day to perform this latest feat. He'd had a bit of Christmas cheer in the form of throat lubricant too. Not that it worried him, driving over the legal limit. Like all cops, he'd be waved through a breathalyser. But it had interrupted his drinking session with the boys.

Back at the station, I was photographed, dusted for fingerprints, sealed in an evidence bag, labelled and locked in Senior Sergeant Robert McKenzie's top drawer. The bad news for Tommy was his fingerprints had been identified on me. Senior Sergeant Robert McKenzie had given up smoking twelve months previously, or so his wife thought. His work colleagues knew better but banded together to keep his secret safe. Technically, he had in fact given up cigarettes, but still enjoyed the odd cigar for relaxation. He kept his addiction hidden from his wife by storing his cigars and lighter in his locked top drawer of his desk at work, the same place I was being held. The cigarette lighter wasn't communicating, as it had died, and the cigars believed themselves superior to pretty much everything in and on the desk, including me, so I was getting nothing from them. I'd done far better with the badge.

I could hear Senior Sergeant Robert McKenzie ordering an underling to ring around the hospitals and see if any burn victims had presented themselves at Emergency. In the meantime, he'd have a cigar while awaiting the results of the calls. He unlocked the drawer, extracted his lighter and a cigar, relocked the drawer and exited the room.

Moments later he returned, swearing, because his 'bloody lighter' was out of gas. He went back to his desk, unlocked the drawer, and went to place the cigar back in its position, but he spotted me in the evidence bag and changed his mind. The prints already taken, no one needed to know he was technically tampering with the evidence as he surreptitiously pocketed me. On the one hand, I was excited about doing my job, but a bit disappointed it was not a cigarette. Just a rotten old cigar with a highly exaggerated sense of self-importance, and the last thing I wanted to do was fire the thing up. But it appeared I had no choice, and I asked myself the now familiar question, 'Will I ever be a real cigarette lighter?'

Outside, behind the building, Senior Sergeant Robert McKenzie enjoyed his cigar. He had carefully placed me in his pocket post ignition, no doubt intent on returning me to the drawer once he had finished. Unfortunately for him, but fortunately for me, this did not transpire.

A young female voice called out to him, "Serge, we've got a hit. A twelve-year-old male presented with burns to his face at Prince Henry's. He's up for visitors!" "Coming!" bellowed the Senior Sergeant. We made our way post haste to the hospital, me forgotten at the bottom of the pocket. Tommy, on pain relief and badly frightened, sang like the proverbial bird, telling all, encouraged by a promise of leniency.

At 11.30 pm that night, Senior Sergeant Robert McKenzie could be found pulling into his driveway, me in tow. He got out of his car and walked heavily inside. Stripping off his smoky uniform, he threw the clothes in the washing machine, set it to wash, hopped in the shower and was soon asleep in bed.

My mind ran rampant as I was pummelled by the swirling, water-soaked clothes. All of the events of the day blurred into one, and as the machine went through the final spin cycle, I wondered whether my flint would ever dry out and whether I would ever be any good again. I lay there till morning, covered in wet clothes and wondering if there had ever been a more sad and sorry cigarette lighter than myself. I did not think so.

The next day dawned bright, promising good clothes-drying weather. Mrs McKenzie, keen to make a start on her chores, opened the lid and began lifting the washed clothes into a basket. With an almighty clatter, I found myself at the bottom of the machine, looking straight into Mrs McKenzie's eyes. She had seen me and was clearly unimpressed. I do not think she was bigoted towards cigarette lighters in general, I think it was more that I represented her husband's deception, and it was that reality that brought the look of disgust to her face. At least, I hoped that was what it was.

Anyway, she scooped me up, marched briskly to the back door, lifted the lid of the wheelie bin and hurled me in, slamming the lid shut. It appeared I was no longer a criminal. I was now trash. My life was going from bad to worse, rapidly. Something had to shift, and soon.

Chapter 8:
Rubbish

I was nothing. Worthless. A failure.

My existence had ceased to have meaning.

I searched inside myself to try to find a spark of hope, of light. There was none.

I had no reason to go on. Discarded, thrown away, gotten rid of, unwanted and unneeded. And yet I had no choice but to keep going, one step at a time, one day at a time.

Lying near the bottom of the bin, I had cause to observe the other occupants. A scrunched-up empty plastic bag that once housed 20 kg of potting mix, a broken toaster, a slightly decaying pair of ancient garden shoes, balled Christmas wrapping paper and a couple of bags of household rubbish, largely consisting of plastic packaging entwined with organic food scraps. We were a glum lot. All destined for the tip. Exposed to the elements, our lifespans would be greatly reduced. We lay there in despair.

The next morning we found ourselves wheeled onto the street, as it was bin collection day. The noisy, smelly truck lifted us high into the air before violently tipping us upside down, where we tumbled onto the mound of refuse already occupying the truck's interior. We rumbled along, settling into wherever we fitted, much like a giant game of Tetris. At each stop, more rubbish would land on us and then settle in until the next load was collected and dumped on us. And on it went until the truck was near capacity. A long drive to the tip followed.

During this, I took the time to try to find any other cigarette lighters. There were a few of us, but the others had all passed on. I was the sole survivor. I felt so horribly alone.

At the tip, the whole lot of us were spewed onto the edge of a giant mound of rubbish as the truck emptied its load. With all the slipping and sliding of everything around me, I could not get a grip on anything and found myself bounced onto the ground, about a metre from the perimeter of the mound. Some other bits of debris were scattered around me, but I had a clear view in all directions. And so I waited.

There always seemed to be some kind of activity at the tip. During the day, trucks and machinery moved piles of refuse around, workers strode purposefully doing their very important work, vermin of all kinds were present day and night, and the flies were unbearable. At times, people, often kids, would come and scour anything of value from the pile that could be sold. These people, like me, had been rejected by their society. Homeless and frequently hungry, they lived in a dilapidated, crumbling old warehouse building. They would gather prized possessions from the tip and take them to a local junk shop, where the owner begrudgingly handed over money for their trash.

Lying on the ground near a dangerous-looking shard of glass, I was spotted one day by one of these people, attracted to my area by the very shiny but otherwise useless shard. She bent down, picked me up and flicked me. I ignited first go. The days baking in the sun had clearly dried me out from my earlier washing-machine drowning. She put me in a grubby reusable shopping bag and continued her searching. An unopened pack of three size 14 women's coloured underwear, a ceramic ashtray, an as-new dog's collar and a box of sickly sweet, cheap incense sticks welcomed me to their midst.

"C'mon!" yelled a voice, barely heard due to the distance between its location and ours and the background hum of machinery. "We're gonna miss the bus!"

"Coming!" she yelled back.

The bus ride was uneventful, save for me developing severe nausea courtesy of the swaying bus and the overwhelming stench of the incense. I was glad to be free of the confined space and odour of the bag when I was dumped onto a counter and under the inquisitive eyes of the junk shop owner.

"What have you got and how much do you want?" he demanded, idly testing me. I passed. Negotiations ensued, haggling ensured, money and goods were exchanged and I, along with my newfound friends, was placed in a basket of miscellaneous items. I had an excellent view.

This shop, unlike the earlier one, was jam-packed with junk. The back of the shop was crammed with second-hand furniture. This only really caused a problem when a customer actually wanted to purchase an item wedged somewhere near the middle. Near the front, the item could be easily obtained. The back wall of furniture had no hope of ever being dislodged or sold, and the items were really only there for display purposes. It was the middle area of furniture that caused the owner the most grief. Cursing, sweating, tugging, pulling, yanking and manipulating the selected piece from its standard position and into the back of a ute or trailer, the owner would congratulate himself on a successful sale.

Out the front of the shop and under an awning was a display of garden furniture, most in need of the odd screw and a coat of paint. A couple of dilapidated lawnmowers completed the scene. The middle section of the shop was largely dedicated to craft supplies. The majority of these craft supplies were literally thousands of balls of cheap imitation wool, found years earlier in a sealed shipping container the owner had purchased, contents unknown and unseen. It had been the acquisition of the fake wool that had given him the inspiration to open his junk shop.

The front of the shop contained the cash register, a small desk supporting a laptop, the more expensive items and anything that could be easily slipped into a pocket. Set up this way, and armed with an eagle eye, the owner had little need for an extensive security system. The shop had frequent visitors, coming to inspect the latest items on display and occasionally a purchase would transpire.

One cold, overcast day, I noticed a priest, dog collar showing, entering the premises. He browsed casually through the new display areas, selecting a coffee mug with the slogan, 'I love the coffee here ... it's the job I can't stand', before heading to the counter.

Glancing in my basket, he spotted me, picked me up and ignited me. "Oh, good. This works," he said to the junk shop owner. "I need a new lighter. My old one is out of gas."

"Didn't think you smoked, Father," commented the owner.

"No, I don't," said the priest. "But I have a little box containing some consecrated communion wafers, a small vial of wine, a candle and a lighter for when I visit the sick. I need a replacement lighter."

And just like that, I had gone from being a bit of rubbish to something of worth. Sure, the priest was not a smoker, which was disappointing, but he had a use for me. I would be used to bring comfort and make people feel better. Very similar to being a true cigarette lighter. I was ecstatic.

Chapter 9:
Humility

The priest turned out to be a lovely man, quietly spoken and calm in nature. Like all Catholic priests, he was unmarried and, with the exception of his cat, lived alone. He preferred it that way. It gave him plenty of time to think, an activity he pursued whenever he had the exquisite luxury of solitude. It was not that he had a problem with people – he found people fascinating. It was just that he preferred his own company and his thoughts to engaging in unnecessary small talk. As a parish priest, he experienced a fair bit of the latter, and so he relished his periods of aloneness. While he shied away from meaningless conversations, he felt it a great privilege whenever a parishioner trusted him enough to unburden themselves to him. He felt honoured and, at times, a bit unworthy of the role, such was his humility. His parishioners adored him because of it. Along with providing spiritual direction at Mass, the Father was equipped with exceptional pastoral care skills.

The bereaved, the sick and dying, the housebound, young mothers with their crying babies, all recipients of his tender care. He would visit, listen as they talked, offer counsel and prayer, and finish up with communion. That was where I came in.

My new home took the form of a hand-carved wooden box with velvet lining inside. Us occupants had our particular places where we lay in the box, the floor having been carved to accommodate our various shapes and sizes. I lay in my little niche, between the candle and the wine vial. The candle holder and container of wafers were positioned where the carver had been able to fit them. It was a fairly tight squeeze, but we all got along well. I thought our home was magical. That was until the others told me almost every Catholic priest had been issued with something similar on his ordination to the priesthood. This news reduced the initial awe I had felt towards the box, but it was still a lovely home.

When the priest administered communion, he followed a set ritual. He opened the box, extracting the candle holder, which was a flat metal circular dish with a hole in the middle, and the candle. He slid the new candle through the hole in the dish and gently placed the apparatus on a level surface. Next came the vial of wine (crystal) and the small metal and glass container of wafers, which were positioned next to the candle. He then opened his prayer book, flipping to the relevant page, and finally removed me from my bed and lit the candle. Prayers, both written and off the cuff, followed. A few drops of wine were dropped on the wafer, which was delivered to either a waiting hand or mouth, depending on the owner's preference. A blessing was performed and, the brief service over, we were packed back in our box, curiously, always in the exact same order we had been removed. It gave me a bit of time to view the surrounds.

The priest loved learning, and most evenings, when there were no meetings scheduled or no one was in crisis, he could be found sitting in his favourite chair, cat on lap, slippers on, devouring some manuscript or book on his favourite topic, St Francis of Assisi. He was obsessed with the man. He wanted to get to know who the man was, what his character was, the kind of man he was. The priest had written three books and numerous academic papers on the life of St Francis of Assisi. Every single person who knew the priest knew of his obsession; it was no secret.

The priest did, however, have a secret, a big one, that he told no one except the cat.

Chapter 10:
The Priest

The priest's other obsession, unbeknownst to his employers, was his fascination with reincarnation. Raised in a good Catholic household, with a healthy sprinkling of both priests and nuns in his extended family, by the time he was on his way to theological college he had fully embraced most of Catholicism's doctrines. A portion of his learning in college was dedicated to the study of other faiths, including Buddhism.

Analysis of these teachings led him to question the beliefs held so dearly within Christianity. He had not felt compelled to terminate his studies, despite his growing confusion, as he was convinced his future lay in ministering to a parish community. And so, mass after mass, he faithfully conveyed the church-approved belief system while secretly harbouring his own doubts. He had other reasons, besides the academic ones, for looking elsewhere to try to find explanations for life's mysteries. As a young graduate, he had experienced a series of dreams. They had one thing in common: they were all set in the distant past.

In some of these dreams, he was male. In others, he was female. In some dreams, he was rich and powerful. In others, he was poor and humble. In some dreams, he was an old person; in others, a young person. Every dream saw him as a different nationality, speaking different languages and practising different customs. The dreams felt very real, sometimes more real and vivid than his waking moments, and certainly far sharper and more detailed than regular dreams. In fact, he could almost recall every one of these dreams some forty years later, in sharp contrast to his regular dreams, which were usually completely forgotten two minutes after waking.

The priest had been convinced for a long time that the dreams were actually memories from past lives. But he had no one he could talk to about this. Virtually everyone he knew would presume he had gone mad, so he said nothing to anyone. He spoke only to the slumbering cat about his musings, usually late at night.

The dream that really stood out for him, though, was one depicting himself as St Francis of Assisi. It was strange. He knew who he was in the dream, but he was in St Francis' body instead of his own. This happened in all the dreams, him feeling like he was in someone else's body, but this time he had a name to go on, an actual historical figure to research. As mentioned, he had developed an obsession with the saint, identifying many shared character or personality traits between himself and the revered man. They shared a deep love of animals and indeed of nature. Their temperaments, from what the priest could ascertain, were almost identical. Both were humble, quiet, calm men. While this alone did not prove anything, there was one other avenue the priest thought worth exploring.

Years earlier, while researching his first book, the young priest had formed a friendship with an older priest, an expert on St Francis of Assisi who worked in the Vatican archives. It was the young priest's deepest desire to somehow gain access to the archives, which stored many unpublished documents and works on the man who became the patron saint of animals. He had mentioned this desire to his mentor, who had recently reported good progress with obtaining the necessary permission to access the archives. He had told the older man he planned to write a fourth book if he could find additional information. What he didn't say was that he was also hoping to access any information the Vatican had on reincarnation.

And so, as one day flowed into the next, life was quiet, usually uneventful and peaceful. I was happy enough undertaking my duties, although on occasions I regretted my lack of experience with lighting cigarettes. I had developed a sense that this was not to be a part of my journey and I needed to be content with what I had. Compared to where I had come from and the other options available to me, this life was fine.

Chapter 11:
Connections

It was about 3.30 in the morning when he got the call. Things had been very slow and steady over the last few months, and the shrieking ringtone of the phone startled him out of his sleep, giving him quite a fright.

"Good morning. Father Brennan speaking."

"Tony, my friend. It's Paul McIntosh. I'm sorry to ring at this hour, but I have just received the news you've been waiting for. I have a permit giving you access to the materials you seek. The permit commences tomorrow and is valid for three months. I am sorry for the short notice, but it was the best I could manage under the circumstances."

The priest, feeling somewhat shocked but also excited, responded with gratitude. "I have been waiting a long time for this opportunity, and now it's arrived. I will wait no longer. I'll be on the next available flight." The two men discussed logistics and plans, and the call was ended.

The priest was ecstatic. For all appearances, he was embarking on an academic journey of discovery. However, he knew his real mission was far more personal. By mid-morning, his flight was booked for that afternoon, bags packed, a locum priest arranged, and explanations made to his superiors. The priest visited his elderly neighbour, a cat lover, who agreed without hesitation to care for his little mate. He knew his cat would be well looked after in his absence. Much to my delight, our little box, with all its contents, was carefully packed in his luggage. I think we were like his lucky charm. He always liked to have a supply of consecrated bread and wine on hand.

Cardinal Paul McIntosh met us at the airport. He had a two-bedroom apartment within Vatican City's perimeter and had offered accommodation to the visiting priest. Depending on the priest's discoveries, the two planned to co-author the book, meaning their living arrangements suited their plans perfectly.

The Cardinal was considered an expert in Church history generally, although his passion lay specifically with St Francis. So extensive was his knowledge that, on occasions, the Pope himself had sought information from him.

It was in this esteemed company I now found myself. I reflected on my life, where I had been contrasted with where I was now. I thought about how all the seemingly unconnected and random events had led me to this point. I had been used for illegal activities and thrown away with the rubbish. I had been responsible for burning human body parts. I had been washed and put out to dry in the sun. I had been party to bringing comfort to the suffering. I had travelled across the globe. I had lit a variety of objects, yet never a cigarette. I held little hope of this dream of mine transpiring within the walls of Vatican City.

And yet, who knew what was around the corner? In life, anything could and does happen.

Chapter 12:
The Transferral

The priest soon established a daily routine in his new environment. Following a morning shower and early breakfast, he would head off to investigate the archives. By mid-afternoon he was back, armed with fresh knowledge acquired from the antiquated documents he was researching. The next few hours saw him madly typing up his notes, followed by dinner with the Cardinal. Over a few glasses of port, the two men would then relax for the evening, amiably chatting about the priest's findings for the day.

The priest had learned quite a bit about St Francis' early adult years, when he had exhibited an adventurous and even mischievous side, according to some acquaintances. The priest recalled his own antics while at theological college at about the same age, reflecting on these additional similarities. He discussed St Francis' character traits with the Cardinal but declined to say anything about St Francis mirroring his own personality so closely. The priest had, so far, enjoyed little success with his other, secret mission. By pure accident, he had stumbled across a document that held some promise. Written by a fourth-century Christian mystic, the author was held in high regard by early Church members. Recognised for his wisdom and intellect, the mystic cited several Biblical passages that allegedly alluded to the existence of reincarnation. Originally destined for canonisation, the document's author was ultimately tried as a heretic, put to death, and his writings forgotten. It wasn't exactly what the priest was looking for, but it was a start.

Meanwhile, I had found myself a temporary new home.

The Cardinal had been required to conduct Mass one morning and, checking his communion box, discovered his cigarette lighter had expired. He had nothing to light the candles with.

"You wouldn't happen to have your box of tricks with you, would you?" he asked the priest. Like that, I had been loaned to the Cardinal.

I didn't mind. It was quite a comfortable resting place, with friendly enough companions, but it wasn't home.

Chapter 13:
Traditions

The news flashed around the globe within moments of his last breath. The fact he was dead was apparent to his physician. The cause remained a mystery. There were a number of possibilities unknown to the public, but the exact reason for his passing would not be confirmed until an autopsy had been conducted.

Every media outlet on the planet interrupted whatever they were doing to blare the news to the world, 'The Pope is dead!'. Our serene, regular lifestyle was catapulted into activity. The Cardinal, called into service, was largely absent from the apartment. Only returning to sleep at night, his days were spent arranging accommodation and other necessities for the anticipated horde of visiting cardinals. Following the death of a Pope, the cardinals from numerous countries were required to gather for the purpose of electing a new Pope. It was tradition. The way it had always been done and what was occurring now.

My Cardinal's role, essentially, was to support the other cardinals, ensuring their needs were met in a timely fashion and that everything ran smoothly for the election. It was a massive job.

The Cardinal had a good staff of workers to assist him in his task, but this did not prevent him from spending hours in tedious meetings. Meanwhile, I was safely tucked away in my box, in the bottom of the Cardinal's briefcase. It was great. I got to hear everything that was going on. The buzz of excitement was palpable and I was infected. This was, of course, tinged with respectful grief for the deceased Pope, but despite this drawback, enthusiasm was high. Like everything religious, the process for electing a new Pope was riddled with tradition.

Following an obligatory Mass, the visiting cardinals were required to meet in the Sistine Chapel to cast their vote. They were locked in, devoid of any contact with the outside world while the ballot papers were completed. These papers were then collected and counted. The successful candidate required a greater than two thirds majority of favourable votes in order to succeed to the position. If this occurred, the ballot papers would be set on fire, emitting white smoke which would be seen coming from the Chapel. This white smoke would tell the waiting millions of Catholics they had a new Pope.

If the result of the vote was less than a two thirds majority, those ballot papers would likewise be burnt, but a chemical added to the fire, causing the smoke emerging from the Sistine Chapel to be black. The message to the world was that the cardinals had not concluded their voting. They would need to repeat the process until they had succeeded in their task.

It was all very suspenseful and highly theatrical.

As things transpired, my Cardinal was to have a very important role in the proceedings. A great honour had been bestowed upon him, no doubt the reward for a lifetime of faithful service. He was to light the taper, a thin, long candle, that would be used to set fire to the ballot papers.

The great day arrived. The cardinals prayed at Mass for a swift decision, then made their way to the Chapel. Locked away from humanity, the cardinals commenced their voting, while the rest of the world took a collective breath, held it, and waited.

My Cardinal, ordinarily quite calm, showed clear signs of nervousness. Nestled in a pocket of the pants beneath his robes, I could feel the blood pumping through his veins faster than usual. He felt hot and sweaty and his voice carried the slightest hint of a tremor when he spoke, which, fortunately for him, was not often.

For much of the time, the Cardinal and I were alone. Tucked in a room, with an enclosed fire box and chimney, we were isolated, just like the cardinals. Complementing the fire box, the scene before us revealed an ornate gold dish that provided a resting place for a dozen or so tapers. Evidently anxious, the Cardinal occasionally reached into his pocket, pulled me out and proceeded to flick me repeatedly. I think he found my flame soothing. This was all well and good, but I could feel my energy draining away. Like the Cardinal, I was nearing the end of my life and after all my trials and tribulations, I wanted to perform one great final act. If the Cardinal did not stop flicking me soon, my great final act would be to fail the Cardinal at a time when he needed me the most. I could not communicate with him to stop. I had no idea what to do.

Chapter 14:
Dying

After what seemed like an eternity, the door swung open. A large, robed cleric marched in, carrying a vessel filled with ballot papers.

"No decision reached. The chemical compound has been added," he intoned, setting down the vessel and commencing the transfer of the papers into the fire box.

My Cardinal selected a taper from the cluster, flicked me, and the taper was lit. The candle was moved to the fire box and bright tongues of flaming paper, intermingling with thick, black smoke, were soon creeping up the chimney.

"Back we go!", said the cleric, cheerfully collecting the vessel and retiring from the room.

Now the work had actually commenced, my Cardinal was considerably calmer and less agitated. The same did not apply to me. I was exhausted. It had taken all my strength to ignite first time. Wrapped in the warm embrace of the Cardinal's hand, I fought to control my growing panic, caused by the thought that I might die before completing my work. I vaguely wondered what would take place if I did not make it and there were still more fires to be lit. What would happen then? Would the Cardinal be able to find another lighter in time? Unless the cheerful cleric was a smoker, I did not think so.

The only hope was that the Cardinal's anxiety returned and he started flicking me again. I would be sure to expire, giving the Cardinal time to locate a replacement while the voting was taking place. However, this did not look likely, as the Cardinal was quite calm and getting calmer by the minute.

It was then that I experienced the strong, quiet thought, "Fear not. What will be, will be. There is nothing to be afraid of". I had the strangest sensation that the thought had come from the fire box.

"Did you just speak to me?" I asked the fire box.

"No, it was not me," came the reply, "it was the fire addressing you. Specifically, the Spirit of Fire, one of Earth's great elements."

Rather than relaxing, I suddenly felt terrified. The Spirit of Fire, the mighty provider of warmth and cleansing, had addressed me, a mere cigarette lighter.

I did not really know how to respond because by now I was absolutely terrified. My thoughts were a jumbled mess.

1. I had, arguably, one of the most important jobs a cigarette lighter had to do, ever. It looked like I was going to fail at my task and severely embarrass the Cardinal to boot.
2. I was dying and had a fair bit of uncertainty about my future.
3. The Spirit of Fire had just addressed me directly and told me not to be afraid.

In my current state, I had not a chance in hell of heeding her advice. All I could do was try to muster both the courage and the energy to respond appropriately when the cheerful cleric next made his appearance.

The cheerful cleric eventually did reappear, with the same news as before and the same vessel of freshly treated ballot papers. I prepared for the inevitable and was able to muster an acceptable flame to pass on to the taper. Again, job done, I lay exhausted in the Cardinal's palm, as the results of this round of voting were conveyed to an eager world, if in a somewhat unorthodox manner.

Flames and black smoke danced together as the strong thought spoke again, "You know you are dying, do you not?"

"Yes", I confirmed.

"You have nothing to fear," spoke the thought gently.

"So you say," I replied, "but from my perspective, it does not look that way."

"What are you afraid of?" she asked.

I proceeded to share my fears and worries with the Spirit of Fire, starting with my anguish at possibly failing to complete this assignment. She told me I was never meant to finish this job. It was not in the agreement.

"What agreement?" I asked.

"The one you made with me before this life began."

"Do you mean I existed before this life?" I queried.

"Of course," replied the Spirit of Fire.

"All fire, regardless of whether it is a raging, life threatening bushfire or a single candle burning, comes originally from me. You and I are one. I am the Spirit of Fire, and so are you. I am all powerful, as are you."

"I see," I replied, although I did not at all.

I was not so powerful when I was discarded as rubbish and was soaking wet. I was not so powerful when I was locked up in a police officer's drawer. I was not so powerful when I was lighting a candle during a communion service. As a matter of fact, I had not shown any signs of being powerful my entire existence. I was just a cigarette lighter who had never actually lit a cigarette. Not once, ever.

The Spirit of Fire, sensing my reservations, softly said, "You were never meant to light a cigarette; it was never your destiny. Throughout your life you were being prepared for a great role, something that will one day change the world, bringing peace and harmony to humanity. When you die, your spirit will join me and together we will travel to your final destination, the Olympic Flame, symbolising unity, hope and ultimately, love. You will join with that part of me that is the Olympic Flame.

You see, I have always been huge, massive, and I needed to experience myself as only a tiny part of my whole being. I needed to be able to relate to all fires, including the humble cigarette lighter, so I became one. In my entire existence I never knew failure. You are a part of me

40

that courageously agreed to experience failure. I am forever in your debt. You are me, just in a smaller body."

I lay there and reflected on her words. Ok, so I wasn't supposed to complete this task. That was good news indeed. Secondly, I now knew what my future held and my fears had been greatly alleviated. I would be absorbed into the Olympic Flame, bringing my experience of failure with me. That was also good news. Finally, I was a part of the Great Spirit of Fire. With that particular piece of good news, I felt my self-worth and self-confidence soar. I was all-powerful indeed. I just never knew it.

The door opened, revealing the cheerful cleric, vessel in hand. "Last one for the day. Same as the other two," he said.

The Cardinal gave me a flick. Nothing. He gave me another flick. Nothing.

"Shake it!" urged the cheerful cleric.

As the violence began, I pushed with all my might, forcing the remaining minuscule amount of gas up the tube. The Cardinal clicked and my final flame ever burned brightly and confidently. It was only brief, but long enough for the taper to light.

"Thank God!" said the two men simultaneously.

Chapter 15:
Epilogue

I was slipping away from my earthly body and moving peacefully and slowly towards a great warmth. Of course, the blazing fire was emitting heat, but the warmth was far bigger than the mere physical sensation, for it was an emotional warmth, welcoming, embracing, enveloping all who could feel its touch. It was strong. It was powerful. It was safe. It was comforting. It was pure love and I had no fear of becoming one with the warmth. When the fire was extinguished, the Warmth and I departed for our final destination: the Olympic Flame. I would reside as part of the Flame for eternity, overseeing the Earth and all her inhabitants. At the precise moment that the white smoke erupted from the chimney of the Sistine Chapel, giving the faithful the news they sought, I united with the Olympic Flame. As one, we would be an unstoppable force. New leaders, including the just-appointed Pope, would rise up to bring transformation to the planet and her people. Wars would cease and suffering would be no more as our Spirit settled across the lands and oceans. Meanwhile, I need to let you, the reader, know what happened to all my friends.

The drug-dealing shop owner was delighted when marijuana was legalised and he was able to peddle his wares publicly and without fear of legal ramifications. He went on to become very wealthy and successful, establishing a roaring trade and employing a team of people, including the four young men involved in this story. Meanwhile, the four young men, now employed and respectable, cleaned up their house and their act and went on to settle down, marry, have kids, and so on. In short, they became conformists.

Tommy, terrified by the injuries he sustained, as well as the fear instilled in him by Senior Sergeant Robert McKenzie, terminated his friendship with the gang. Lauded as something of a hero among his peers, he started to like school a bit better and apply himself. As it turned out, Tommy was exceptionally gifted and, in later life, would play a crucial role in disease prevention and elimination. Tommy's mother wrote a book about the trials and tribulations of raising five children as a sole parent. The book garnered significant interest, becoming a single mother's Bible, and Tommy's mum found herself able to quit her job, living off her book sales and rearing her five children with much less stress. Of course, Tommy's changed behaviour assisted considerably with this as well. Because Tommy had been injured in the fire and was so frightened, the magistrate let him off lightly. It was also recognised by the court that Tommy had most likely been heavily coerced into participating in that day's events.

The magistrate, however, was not so lenient with the other four boys. They were ordered to engage in community service at the school where the fire had occurred. It did not sound like much of a punishment, but each boy was required to attend their placement ten hours per week until the age of sixteen. The magistrate justified the punishment by saying it would give these kids less free time to act up. The school principal was delighted, the cop was satisfied, and the boys were devastated. The punishment worked though. While all their friends were playing and partying like regular teenagers, they were forced to grow up and behave like adults. It steered them away from future delinquency.

Senior Sergeant Robert McKenzie and his wife separated following a massive argument about him smoking. There were obviously other underlying issues, not least of which were his deception and her nagging. It was an appalling marriage where they brought out the worst in each other. They were both much happier a few years later with their respective new partners and new lifestyles.

The junk shop owner and the homeless people at the tip had an unexpected and related windfall. One day, scrounging amongst the rubbish, a zip-lock bag with several coins inside was unearthed. The shop owner had the coins analysed by an acquaintance and they were found to be highly valuable. The shop owner sold them privately to avoid detection by the authorities. Knowing this, the homeless people demanded sufficient money from the shop owner to set themselves up in something a bit more permanent. He complied but kept a good portion for himself. He was never detected by the authorities.

The priest co-authored his fourth book on St Francis of Assisi, having discovered new material about the man. His belief that he was indeed the reincarnation of the famed Saint grew stronger and he applied for and was granted permission to have permanent access to any material within the archives related to reincarnation. He became a bit of an expert in the field and the new Pope, open-minded and curious, frequently sought him out for updates on the progress of his research and findings. The cheerful cleric left the Church to marry his assistant, an equally cheerful woman who made him laugh. The Cardinal co-authored the book with the priest but died before it was released. His input was appreciated by the hierarchy and his name became synonymous with taking care of and paying attention to detail. Loved by many, his legacy lives on.

And so, I come to the end of my tale. It has been an incredible life of ups and downs, highs and lows, and isn't that just what life is about?

Footnote

I first had the idea to write this story about 20 years ago. A cigarette lighter, with the name 'Grand Hotel, Darwin', had come into my possession. It had been given to me by a friend who had "borrowed the lighter from someone at a party and never given it back!" It got me wondering how a cigarette lighter had made its way from Darwin to Melbourne. I wondered how many hands it had passed through and what things it had experienced.

And thus, the idea for the story was born. Thank you for reading it. I hope you've enjoyed this little tale as much as I've enjoyed writing it.

—Cath

Cath Cunningham

46